Corey Wakeling | The Alarming Conservatory

New Poems

GIRAMONDO POETS

Corey Wakeling | The Alarming Conservatory

First published 2018
from the Writing & Society Research Centre
at Western Sydney University
by the Giramondo Publishing Company
PO Box 752 Artarmon NSW 1570 Australia
www.giramondopublishing.com

Designed by Harry Williamson
Typeset by Andrew Davies
in 10/16.5 pt Baskerville

Printed and bound by Ligare

Distributed in Australia by NewSouth Books

Cataloguing-in-Publication data
is available from the
National Library of Australia

ISBN 978-1-925336-61-0 (pbk)

To George Wakeling,
autodidact of camera, aircraft,
and conservatory
1930–2017

He took you for a bubble gum American,
But now he finds that you speak kangaroo English.

BARISTA AT THE HAMBURGER BAHNHOF IN BERLIN

Contents

Agora, Arcadia

Hardest of places to begin the blueprint, chewed cuticles
To the gristle bone-white, stertorous the drafts that make up
Our permanence tethered and forever.
Agora Arcadia the molar cud.
Most of anxiety is about hoarseness and the wizened
Subgenre, which spurts like a geyser but stinks like all
Rudimentarily. Anxiety does well to refer to itself as per norm.
The double standard of proclaiming reading
And disclaiming citation as you rarefy the fixed image.

My 1992 Camry Twin Cam still rots in shop,
But Walliston's last garage is now a bush kiosk.
Affiliations so splay they rustle like departing company
Through the privet, which is theirs, my ghost gums weeping.
Sullen roadside demeanour in the successful suburbs.
Nature strip: you are lucked fiendish; no Frigidaire.
High Wycombe's new Coles is starchy, but tending its own
Mistral. Not behind thee, but before me, formaldehydry.
'[F]rom my crawl and from their crawl', and was the
Snivelling limited to the thin one? I see a balled-up human
unlimited, must be unhappy in some way.

What have I been party to?
The bongs are not what they seem. Psychology is a mutant
Of fandom closed-circuit. Newquay = Portsea.
The coast I forget.
The Perth craze is easiest in me when kiting and the fishermen
At Fremantle get blowies. No sardines for us. You're
Inedible in the dark, but stern. You're often furniture in the
Ferns, you know. Betray my Ben Bulben, Camry,
Exhibition with surgery the phonetics are nursing we'll be
Arcadia-scared again, I promise, though my village be captured.

Odes to Parkville

1

Amusing that a yonder ghost world of brackish
love becomes hagiography. We will the power
to forget Lubbock, to look towards a panoptic
New York, which pops or does not, whose height
omniscient is the spectral hiss nescience
of a march in theory. Five seconds Parkville.

2

Southside of Fitzroy Town Hall. Four children
with anamorphic adult legs, petulant at an angle,
one bike and a basketball. '[T]owards a panoptic / New York'
'the uneasy accommodation to self implicit',[1]
my green shoulder collapses
and I take the rotten marrow bone home to bury.

---

1 Mary Bryden, *Women in Samuel Beckett's Prose and Drama: Her Own Other*, Palgrave Macmillan, 1993, p.131.

3

'[W]ill the power / to forget Lubbock,'
says Mum, her skiff collapsing.
All the bayous splinter in remorse, orange sonnet,
and indemnity pays for a return to a fruitful zero
which warrants Plum Duck at Green Field.
Cricket's started again.

4

Royal Park detains two immoveable statues
the Wheel of Fortune dizzies.
The crawling man has a bifurcated nose
which is apology enough, pavement's blood
by night dances even when it is still,
'not ... whose height / omniscient is the spectral'

5

North Melbourne, 'a march in theory',
denounces the traitorous shoulder levy
and I do think we will dodge it
for the last five seconds we're granted.
The plum duck pauses to compare glycerine
with the snot of the fallen among sulphur eucalypt.

6

A children's hospital is a solemn thing,
really, even when the fourth of July is televised
to the dark morning lit, strung, by a system
of LEDs and the coughs of hot ballooning.
'[S]econds ... Parkville ... \\ pops or does not',
the unremembering plaques of a hospice.

7

Does eight equate to two deaths not averted
at the halfway house, asks the torso's
'power / to forget', that artisanal forge in which
correspond all these blood relations
more rotten than some craven morning half-lit
with solemnity and its strangers.

8

Friendship's autumn is a catastrophe preventative
when we boast it with fireworks. Pity each
firework already has a patron. '[A]musing that this
long / hagiography' is a nation's keeper
when it's you I love more than the floor.
Look, it's the bike path which leads to the casuarina

9

I hung from my wrist from it, to disappear those hours.
What. Ask epiglottitis for a more permanent stay
in Brunswick, my optimism is a nuisance, 'nescience
/ of a march', even to my version of memory,
which is a last tantrum in a city glade
which reminds most of a desolate Hampstead Heath.

10

Poor old savage club, poor geriatric mercy.
The district is just another kind of elegy.
All those fingers lost in the dirt, and crane boulevard,
the many patrons of landscape. '[A]musing'.
The hand here admits it feels every newcomer
approaching. That's one definition of anxiety.

11

They are already prospecting what niche will take
your cadaver as the tumescent meantime swells
aloft an etherised skyline.
'[L]ook towards a panoptic New', and those pleasure
craft that are deaf to mercy, memory, suggest you and I
watch a chameleon ideology on iview.

12

What is that eye in the dirt. Patronage.
Firework frenzy and the launch of two Sydney-bound
adventure narratives. I often think of poor, porous
Marcus Clarke. But think of Shillinglaw:
'nautical to a degree in his phraseology
as well as a most 'robustious' singer of 'chanteys'[2]

---

2 *Australian Dictionary of Biography*, MUP, 1976, Volume 6.

13

More. 'Hydrographer to the British Navy'[3]
a chant of Basque Country remembered on a Ryanair
serviette to Barcelona is lamington subsistence not for long.
Anyhow, romance shines in my eyes, they say, deplete
'brackish'. That swoon in the hay was less tantrum than mantra,
and had I cultural amnesia I would return to Ukraine.

14

The impossible memory I want to bring to our kindergarten.
Yes, romance is a kind of science fiction, one way or another,
I admit. The type of gossip which returns
the promised friendship band not to mercy
but to nursing is as robust as a stripling in a storm.
'Five seconds' straight I have talked straight.

---

3 'Death of Mr. J. J. Shillinglaw', *The Argus,* May 1905.

15

What were they doing in Royal Park without the river,
the pine needles, and the birch wood? Tagine has waylaid
the river of mouthfeel. What elegy for the patron
'nescience is'. Levies continue to keep the march
from belonging. Window shopping, however, is an invitation
for every stranger, precisely the hallowed global usher.

16

Happy Birthday, you massacre. And where is that loot
you promised me. Cane toad symptomology
for future concealment, but 'to look towards a'
crazy robustness still makes for slow cantering up the parade.
Sutra, elegy, or otherwise, the serviette fictions are amazing.
Topography wins documentary. Fast the eye.

Are Forever

Nothing reverts to nous when we disinter dead poets,
because of the death quandary. Although, not economical.
But, like the anvil, which is extinct too,
kerosene vagrancy at the mint becomes a prison,
and even at the end of times the bureau
is something to catch your reflection, in beneath bedroom's
velvet proscenium and silk drawstring for the Swan's entrance.
But can it be sterile long enough, father enterprise.
It can be hokey if alienated enough from the strip.
Can it even turn back to innovation, daredevil.
I am too rich for this. But being faceless is the virtue
of my Aussie head. Virtue makes faceless beauty,
in effect. Bogus and sour duration when entitlement
Brobdingnagian and State-implemented has no fiction.
If it were so towards a supreme fiction it would not be
so possessed of this world. How tired is cocaine,
after all, but it is not your nausea, pupil, yours is that
you do not decode your reading. No more marathons,
he decries, a farce of a baptism anyhow and never a place
for repertory. I may fail the tests of paronomasia to enlist here.
Childless bureau debates ethics like a burp,
farts soaking the shabby plaster of affectionate cages
to spirit, pity's sake, which is here encapsulate.
No spirit which is not anvil, death, reflection,
sound waves and pupae in this pestilent diamond undivided.

Reactor of the Tiny Minutes

Space of relief is space left,
    because stimulants were always in the armoire,
even if that's the elegant boys' room. How long is
    childhood. Atomic thud reverberant. Chide in bristly
portions and accident intervals,
    like old masters who turned out to be cacti,
probably insurgent disruptions,
    because beyond the mountains a bothersome American
TV station keeps borrowing indiscriminately
    our uncited phrases which themselves stray from
the registry. Can this departure suggest better hours between
    those consonants. The cute stuff wins.
    He was a plasterer until he found electricity.
Then he became that hydroelectric plant.
    The background radiation of your average US state.
But the stones can't be seen what with the avenues
    of bathrooms and smoking. The mist as we approach
curdles. Then, relief. There are brains between immemorial
    grill, but like the open crypts of the powder years,
Pearl Harbour | 1503 | the long red nose
    as the myth that returns as electricity embanked
in the smoke, which compacts the ikea city, stains
    reactionary racism in checking the edibility of a native
seaweed. To finally discover you are a racoon
    has its perks. Like that we love each other
accidentally and still, though I appreciate canon's hair-raising

oral tradition in those northside bars we envy,
it is enough to fish again in the morning and nightmare.
Perforce I don't feel hungry.
A challenged onion is sweetest. Fruit of plains.
They. And the labourer inside I reserve
for some testosterone certitude of the hairline.
The seduction of symmetry glazes a gravure cloaca,
makes gorgeous floor tiles around it, meaning we can win.
We can win dignity when it is up for sale. Due anxiety
returns to due entrepôt, preface, like gravy on chips
at the sports carnival. Mum has Dad on the phone,
extricating the workplace from the fashionable spirit,
say, though camellia turns a phrase no matter what
he says and the Dobermans still have their leashes
in their teeth.
So really speak your mind. Yet do you.
Be glad to be elsewhere. In love, relief is the thing itself,
flowers or otherwise. Somehow in outrage of gladness
that we both knew this is captivating, purposive
nonstop, the dwarf star leaves traces on the chassis
and with our meal, the redness of goodness.
We both knew this and know this, this being that
nothing converts some virgin time.

Charlatan

You say you want to end the charlatan, yet
yours is the standstill cruciform bleak daylight
saved evening, starkly
scapegoated. *See*, you say, *sign*
of the bold made prone. Glad there
the vanity at the Dandenong soak, your tight
grip, it is a secret during the Australian Open
commentary, which is pointless.
Sloth number in the lamb, but an avid mind
before the end. Avid subject supine
our bascule. Snap my back. In the sedge gulags,
Captain Cook nod, Marcus Clarke wet,
rubicund like the infant
coast, spry not fey beyond gambling.
You would shoot it. Wheedlers in the elderly
club by the ancient pub.
May I add that not all chance is wrong.
Do not let it, is the numerary signal.
Variations: I suck the bullets
useless. Poorer country and rabid distractions,
fey was always spry she-oak but duly noted
and our bascule supine.
Captain Cook 'disappeared' with gold galoshes.
Betrayal of missing persons. Which of us
at sea really survives the salt?

Epicure

Why are they curious. Surely
they know how much we hate them.

Return the Yankee bust.

The Geelong pass might just be my pilgrimage,
if I can convince all the province's nurseries.
The small person grove is bordered by
persimmon and land-marked with gum.
The full-bore ethics as we loiter.
Famous noble incest elopes from real estate for gulf,
wiping clean the bust of the ruin-discovered Victoria
from the empty lot, because it's maladapted
to our future cabinet. No geometry to the chisel
given blunt hands. Though they must,
the Darling Ranges don't appear to end anywhere,
but instead thicken with industry and suburbs
southward. Yankee recurs in persistence,
but they have no business with your fate,
fair acedia. Jury duty upon recent court appearance,
hence *known*, Queen Street slander at the window.
No way out, it appears, some time to come.
Nero and Narcissus are always with us.
Prolong esperance for the discussion of Korean

divides, later the Antarctican, new European republics,
but I think the Australians will win,
will sentence, with the yardstick still whittled
to toothpicks. I am optimistic about
the mutual fruits of our poverty and celebrate
the present and its imaginative fetor.
Gum descent persimmon protect.
Child, if they do not understand you but
in the pig pen, maybe shit hurling beats
intimation, sermon in that grove of children.
More Plato than Aristotle it seems,
De Anima promises.
Beauty being the outward appearance
of Truth, how to get
to the head of the dynasty
by convincing the epicure
to poison him?

Pupils of the Goat

Following tradition, we name him Australia.
Australia stays clear of the electric fence.
Hoofs praise dandelion chaos and blackberries
stammer like a lathe, drolly giving guns goals.

The Bibbulmun was infernal to all our feet,
especially the kid straggling during the commute.
Is there really nothing minatory
about having to gamble. Dunno.
We decide to play chess at each milestone
of the kid's shadow's beeline. The excursions.
Our break at midday when we hit the ferns.

What would I do if I had to gamble and play chess
changing his clout over tense pastures.
Albany, you might say is heaven,
Kalamunda calls itself hell.
They honeymoon in the shadows and the ferns.
Darling Ranges make a really arbitrary purgatory,
so purge, confess, or okay the escape.
Confessions of the clean clout or the oven
are not forthcoming, because to betray love
reveres exile. Don't ask Beatrice alone, ask me,
face-to-face. Unclench your fists. Holy cataract.
Reactionary, the clearance of the émigré
is always unclear. Haunches

dribbling spun over. Upbraid the braiding
stile aloft, maybe never. None of us
are high jumpers, jumbucks, equestrians.
Have ever. The old Corolla couldn't jump,
nor could the Celica or the Datsun.
You bit the armpits off the Datsun,
hence no one had anything
to hold on to. You did this as a kid.

Car encapsulates red and yellow,
the flowering eucalypt pouring into our prison.
Though never sunburnt in here,
sunburnt by the glass and steel
of the city out there. During our hip hop
education, sitters too were having Australians.
Tupac seems forever like a fading still.

Scary chalk circle defined by the summer's
midday melt when all you
want to be is nursed healthy. It is chilling,
though, back on the path, the marri unwarped
by imagination or the wind,
stolidly opposed to the wind and the kids,
no low branches to climb up on,
a skin of scales painful to grip.
It's late afternoon now and his shadow is long,
his festering paranoia ripens, and now the endgame
is a blinding migraine as the employment stakes heighten.

What idea would fertilise the Darling Ranges,
Purgatory, Bickley's orchards and grasses,
Mundaring's reservoir uninterested, the car overheating,
hissing, the swaddle enlarging,
the shadows multiplying sibilant like a gulley,
during the dreams of divorce.

Confess. I notice no confessions forthcoming from the company,
ferns or babysitters, without the curiosity to get lost,
more concerned with the crown and the changing of clout.

The apples, ripe in fester, explode in their lofts,
the cars stricken until husk, the most arbitrary of the range
flooding by its gland the weir. The sun is black but all is black.
All encumbered with bodies in a heartland sod.

Tell me: what is dirt and what is water.
Here there is no telling for sure.

Air becomes ether by the rot, Albany,
the escape memorial, downs the flight of stories.
All clout and south-facing.
The promontory is an eye.
The cars overthrow themselves with the bodies.

———

Remember the Australians.

There is confession in us face-to-face struck dumbly,
Katherine Prichard's bauxite ledge,
all Greenmount spinning like a comet,
which fits with national legends of failed speculation.
Your asbestos teeth merge with my flesh, capillary field
forever, some kink in my heart a fat nerve *sui generis*.

No, the unfed wildflower obloquies
eucalypt flowering black.
Levitating, sure, but mid-air floating,
Pandemonium all the Sterling.

Your minders are still having Australians,
and stills have simply become another effect of montage.

What is the difference after all
between swamp, migraine, and blindness.
The unclimbable and the untouchable. Yes –
squint.

Notice the kid fallen dead like a prophet,
no purge but instead a finale. Fine, a resolution:
the difference between a kid and a lamb
is one is a goat. And goats have advisors, not pupils.

Ward

A testing ground for what is not pasture is a ward.
He shirks the cool of morning's impatience,
even upbraids your proximity beyond the daisies,
by the empty cop shop. At your peril,
seethes suburb's bush.

No hiking to and from the Yu Yangs.
More like crawl. Incoming purple the herald of retreat.
A blue ribbon cuts a rising auburn from purple
and a strip of gold
and from the history of escaping by train.
Homecoming. Hot road balm substitute.
No trace of coast, but close.

Inside, the couches intrigue by a slow invitation
which becomes entrapment.
The Essendon subsistence is a cultivated jaundice,
you know. We enjoy not being
happy together. It is high drama
by comparison with high tea, when we used to visit
the CBD for loathing and the ceramic.
For pavlova.

Present. The tsunamis were a surprise,
and that they came in acts, rather than scenes.
We inlanders exempt from chaos short-lived.

Punished my daughters for marrying
outliers, then enjoyed the exile of spurious urbanity
as Jaques. To an anomie of knowledge marinates
my fool-glad solitude. The voice of you-know-who.
This kind of learning was mostly Midas-inspired,
an effort to gild a flight from failure
with the inevitable lapidary, the constant reminder
of Albert Namatjira, who is the only immediate rescue
here and now from the couches.
The saluting couches. The car, prone on the respirator,
wheezes demand during the equanimity
of commute. Hard patience is cruel living.

All the images of rejuvenation are diversion –
sex, devotion, enterprise –
and the face still pestilent, its pocks
the warm caves for labyrinth virulence.
The mouth is no fun when dry,
and especially not when only scaffold and strut,
steel and concrete,
open and closed.

The houses begun in the head in that post-tsunami
dramaturgy of the world flourished.
Like a couch, the advantage is earned by those
who sit with you to console and comfort themselves.
Then that exploitation cinema of entrapment
and suspense, the always exile horror, invites in turn,

to turn in talc and float in the vapours
of an absent amniosis of a perpetual broken
neck of universal self-presence.
It means focus your gaze into the lens to distract
from romance off-camera.

How is it all of them survive, including you.
Of course there was that beachside dais
which let all the water through
but crushed its offensive rebound, and sky of course
was cut to let all of that land through
and its haze of talc. But nothing was born of foam
or fluid, dirt or danger. The houses were mostly
lonely, incarcerated to each other by the hyphens.
The light remained reclusively Albert Namatjira.

I wonder how Buladelah rethinks this capacity,
that lunar selector!
His dam the alien waters trespassed,
between what he preserves and what he does not.

How about take my Fairlane down to Bunyah
into the tallowwood and make a crypt of the trees.
From the purview of death, how about I
watch the dam drain to a wrinkle, and, in turn,
transform into a withered eye closed.

The tree limbs encourage the anthropoid,
the anthropoid bits of an alien catastrophe
of the periscopes, all the Homeric sagas
made Martian, and refashion high idleness
into three major poetic games of fencing
between homestead and land, what
ensconced in hinterlands to urban centres
across a landmass name country
Country.

The counter. Count the wild rye,
wry eye of Country.

Yes, I will be too dead for the dashes
of a mud corpus become certain,
too dead for fencing and agriculture.
Instead, sat in the creases of an eye,
dreams dreams as ward of state.

Elegy Written in a Dead Metropolitan Library

Prefer the virtual ceilings of turnpikes and mountains
and stay put for change. Let the gravitational reversal come.

It's laughable season of family unity, and tempest
in the yuletide spondee, 'past dark'.

Cheap lamentations but for pointing out the sun
by the above-ground poolside glitter Jung preserves.

What are Maida Vale dispensations, the approach like this
\\\

the departure like that //

the jewels, though shaken, elude the international
syndicate who had our bounty on their list? So, for now,

the shade, four seasons delicately rocked, the panda
breeding itself off the endangered list,

the fox, now stifled at the turnstile and chemically castrated,
beloved.

You are now all our friends, climate servile,
laughable or tempest.

My shadows come to your apartment and move your furniture
for you. It's easier tossing your furniture from the slate,

it pulverises better. I like that your telephone stand is obsolete,
it will keep my microwave company.

Maida Vale is so rude when it hears of your tranquillity,
the calm come after tragedy. How many Christmases have you

missed? Yes, all the pseudonyms we can use for you that won't
sound like euphemisms, because the apartment has relieved you

and the redundancy package is indefinite.
For service to the implacable sunshine, even the international

crime syndicate takes you off their list, my shadows steal
your bike, and Christmas has come again.

Your entombed library of undead things is screeching now.
International law shrugs. Sure, the electric wire won't mute

the screams, but Tesla would be proud of the field of shock
even Edison would realise if he tried to take a piece

of this partition. Don't they know how happy the tranquillity
of the relief of catharsis of tragedy of future of calm is,

the company kept of shadows innumerable where London delights,
the tailored spines and the tempered promise and the tapered

bounty of your super?
And so a demiurgic suspicion for the ice-land of your peace

looks sillier still when departure is prolix
and you contemplate a seaside life, if only to be the cargo

of your fugitive, the demon of chance stuttering his free advice
which is plagiarised from a lost poet's grave,

which it is my obligation to share with you, here verbatim:

burying your library confirms its tenure,
vermiform it does not ensure a future.

Ombudsman Reader

An acceleration to good news not Fairfax nor News Corp but
A spectacular slap to the jowl, Australian reader.
We all went to Oxford but then took Auden's class at Michigan
During which he dreamed his departures. There are many:
Some national, some intellectual, some formerly private.
Yes, how many British sowed cattle prods
In the rural on the Eastern seaboard of America,
Which we weren't capable of, furniture removalists to Pembroke
Being, and others, when not in Oxford, a side quid
On bare knuckles. We rap the knuckles ourselves, hoping
They'll hear us. The Australian vanity that sent them there,
A vanity Joyce and White called cracked looking-glass;
If only it were smashed up more, for a window on the backboard.
Hope the late-blooming pervert too savages the selfie trend
Of a funereal canon. Lazarus might have dug himself out
but how about a lazar house. Wounds, cankers, sour jaundice:
Scratch and roast, then buy yourselves back as volumes,
Because my bookshelf lain bare and my still unfashionable kids
Need some dollars for heating in this cool miner's cottage.
Fed, ombudsman reader instead settles
Into the stone bench outside by the wayward daisies
And the monument waratah, behind which the hagioscope,
A view of the persistent roughage of this poverty.
Identifying scales of the epistolary overdraft, the illicit frown.
The contracts to local council remit, but fain class anyhow,
Which the family tries to conceal with jam trees,

Which are never privet. Where is the privet I can't see the forest
For, anyhow? Happiness can usurp affirmation, which still makes
Of the colleges a briny rhetoric for self-presence
And self-preservation. What you called salty, once upon a time.
When we're beef steaks, how soon Indonesia,
Because knowing the primeval inhale of all metallic alarms,
Fate of the hagioscope head, if it has its own gestures,
Might drink in the evaporated.
Artisan automata mechanic familiar uses the word
'Breatharian', which is likeable on the East coast,
Since it has little Masonic origin, whereas get further south
And you might have protests against your Rosicrucianism.
The caravan has cruised all day without interruption,
Notwithstanding magpies, and if we keep pushing
We'll make it to camp in time for the burials.
Surrounded by a goat herd whose landscape feed is replaced
With corn, we know what this does to their eyes:

It turns them red waratah. Speechless, reader.
Do not eat what aspic preserves.

Alfresco Dining Area Dining Alfresco

The alfresco dining area shrinks as the couple sprint, the alfresco dining area
sandwiches as the opposing alfresco amazes, which is the amazement of the
hegemonicon cited in a choral splurge which the alfresco dining area sublimates.
Prologue to parliament's legislation, passed from federal to state to *ipse*,
to expand the alfresco dining area. I sit in the alfresco dining area
looking for the alfresco dining area, which can't be seen for the alfresco dining
area, which as some kind of aquarium effect must be some kind
of alfresco dining area effect of the aquarium which is an effect
of a pre-existing alfresco dining area. It must be some kind of terrestrial
enormity, so predictable I can only sit in it, not see in or of it.
The alfresco dining area whimpers when the Rottweilers come,
barks when the cats, drools when the birds and whispers
when the humans, which the humans cannot see for the humans.
The alfresco dining area whistles with the wind, solders with the heat,
burnishes with the wax and sighs with the caress. The alfresco dining area
can't come indoors, I protest, which the alfresco dining area protests

for the liberty writ unto its name, which is its protest and outdoor
remains, which is itself the alfresco dining area outdoors protesting
which is its freight to the traduction of the name alfresco dining area.
Given a trapdoor, the alfresco dining area is a trapdoor alfresco dining area.
Given a liquor license, the alfresco dining area is a licensed alfresco
dining area. Given an eviction notice, the alfresco dining area
is an evicted alfresco dining area. Given a crowd, the alfresco dining area
is a crowded alfresco dining area. Given a loft, the alfresco dining area is
an alfresco dining area aloft. Given a basement, the alfresco dining area
is an alfresco dining area based. It does not help to give, but does
it help to punish. Punish the alfresco dining area by minding your own business
indoors. Punish the alfresco dining area
by transferring its management's balance to a competing financial
institution without its knowledge, dissolve its ownership.
Punish the alfresco dining area by flouting its
border by jumping its queue or drinking alcoholic beverages
outside of its perimeter purchased inside it. Punish the alfresco
dining area by ordering food from a competing restaurant

by flagging down a competing waitperson and pretending that you
are sat wrongly, that the host sat you there.
Punish the alfresco dining area by astral plane or daydreaming
your transplantation. Punish the alfresco dining area by not
dining.
Punish the alfresco dining area by dining without the area.
Punish the alfresco dining area by levitating,
flouting the terrestrial markers of the alfresco dining area.
Punish the alfresco dining area by swimming. When evicted,
confuse the alfresco dining area by beginning an original alfresco
dining area in a Venn diagram overlap with the alfresco dining
area.
Confuse the alfresco dining area by waiting on your table and
dining
at your customer's table. Confuse the alfresco dining area by dining
on yourself, not by yourself. Confuse the alfresco dining area by
licensing
your own liquor within the alfresco dining area. Confuse the
alfresco
dining area by installation of prisms at the vertices of its
perimeter.
The hegemonicon of the alfresco dining area reasserts itself
by collapsing its loft and filling in its basement, by plastinating
the crowd, by patenting the perimeter of the area, by force
feeding
the plastinated crowd, by vaporising the excess, by a trigonometric
archive of the final limits of the alfresco dining area, by the

universal preservation of the trigonometric archive of the final limits

of the alfresco dining area in the human genome, by the reificatory
universality of the universal preservation of the trigonometric
archive
of the final limits of the alfresco dining area in the human genome,
by the final temporal guarantee of the reificatory universality
of the universal preservation of the trigonometric archive
of the final limits of the alfresco dining area in the human
genome
in an alfresco dining area of the final limits of the trigonometric
archive of the universal preservation of the reificatory
universality
of the final temporal guarantee of its area
dining alfresco, or:
alfresco dining area dining alfresco.

Elegy for Epithalamium

My mishearing is the beginning of the truth:
the weir is forecast full. Gangsters are the first to evacuate,
and they take all the cars. We spoke a lot about getting our own.
The only make we could agree on was a Datsun Mum
loved but forgot once in a secret parking lot called Australia.
Anyhow, the cost of extortion to the hydrolectric station
in this satellite town is high. Our lozenges, also for
soreness, we saved for a formidable registry.
Limestone edges make soft cicatrix all our friends make
of their tenure not our time. The rise of that bloatsome weir
kills sleep, all the thunderous organs we learn to ignore
now that the gangsters are gone. The bus routes have stopped.
I am caged happily at your ear.

There is a death in my half of the bed, which smells
of Melbourne's truffle hunt. Hence the bloodhound
gets euthanised. I take up an ethical animal
to replace him: some crippled foundling whippet.
Debate for the plains' secession from the outer rim
and to merge with the eighth circle leads most debates
to pub urinals, where depending upon addition or retraction
of a clause I either bite the porcelain, if it is old, or break
my teeth on it, if new. My half of the bed brushes his teeth before
sitting in the rain in Royal Park a lobotomite. Distant traffic.

The Children's Hospital is a fluorescent sibyl, her gas
the incinerated sheets. I put my ring finger in my mouth
and suck till it's chaffed and shows a red ring
where that wedding might have been, where the cigar cutter
should go, Robespierre. Danton!

To have been on Station Street all this time tugging at his beard
bouncing on his knee and pouring his beer into his America's Cup,
the froth might have foreseen the brimming of the weir.
Electrolysis is not hydro with the next affidavit, which secures
a homelessness that the gangsters will not repeal,
not even as the Queensland State Government bullies its own
infrastructure, which I envy, since the home made of minutes,
nevertheless without pieces, remains a chessboard,
which I can still play.
Won't ever again beat genius except by a premeditated charge
which, for three moves of the game, has a contingency
of three moves, so long as genius is predictable
and wears his fez and the cord hangs west.
I have him mate. This sounds like marriage.
Yet, when with the final roll of the dice you shake your head
and the cord of your tress turns east – the morning the weir's
sputum defeats me – neither you nor I checks mate in sight.

Our little Sandrino is three years old but will not outlive the flood,
but what do I know
thumb in mouth and fucking my way to the splendid city of Milan.
All of their gum trees are odd there, so, as Sandrino gets grief-sick
from the foregone conclusion the Children's Hospital states
on the weir's nearing lava flow,
it's more enjoyable this prospect of greeting hell on earth
with open arms for safe passage to the humble fidelity of subjects.
Grief: my fidelities ever brand new the infidelities
to your ear, which caught fire with that perimeter of peppermints
that once ensconced us perfume.
You aspired to a glorious facility where my dreams
meant international diplomacy.
But there is no ark big enough to withstand a warrior overflow.

Vertigo at the diving board to caldera my grandfather built
of alluvial jarrah and the carpet of an unborn chin. Burnt
peppermint cloak of truth I wear to bed the night before,
after the rehearsals, which will stain this dais forever, is my hope.
Because if eternity won't be mine I hope I can stain memory
eternal. We will not sleep. I cannot sleep, in vertigo.
Diplomacy is shelved in the translation archive of Australia,
below the parking lot, where it's supposed to be funny
that the colonnade is in the shapes
of hourglasses.

On the burnt Nakasendo and with floodwaters kilometres below
at the foot, Matsumoto Castle is only its top tier
peering out to offending sea like a beach shack.
Here they propose, the tea fields aren't going to get any greener.
It's summer, the swollen cicadas howl impressive dissent,
demanding return to diplomacy with the interior empire,
independence. You fling wide your arms and make the shape
of the quincunx, a five in the dice roll, which suspiciously
confirms an eternity. Your lips make a zero,
which is not on a die, and kiss my idiot tears.
A farmer in fluorescent galoshes laughs at wedded trek
up a sluice, tells us home is posterior.
Of course it's history's farmer laughing down ascent to the peak.

Milan is as empty of jobs as the Nakasendo.
The Children's Hospital is one of few antediluvial things,
a sensorium of neon is the zero future.
All silence to all embassies, the wedding guest is this weird
passport whose photo is the two together.
Unstamped embossed pages. Numbers replace where there would
be letters, letters replace where there would be numbers,
the hologram under the light the lucent shimmer of each other's
ghost. Wife's husband and husband's wife entwine.
Demon games at the supernaculum chewing biltong each

in an enemy's likeness. The charred etching of bodies in the futon.
A wall of hygiene is unheard but looks like the horizon when it
hits. At this timeless punctum, all soaks sibyl.
After the heat, it hardens into an archive of sand time.
Ice bath Carlton is no warrior.
The archive is a conservatory for which cicadas are the chorus,
and it is so like occupation in this shattered stillness as an idiot.

New Fruit

How much you are with them in the crowd is still a question.
I can make this better for our family.
The world's new fruit rots. On the ground this is incense.
If we fake it, might we fool them. When they're fooled
Are they forever ours. Rest assured, they are forever fooled
And ours, so no use in calling the inevitable
A question. Let the tongue harden in the mouth as a monument,
For a greater good is the concrete of our mouth.
Thanks for your involvement in the fires and recovery, Australia.
I forgot which you are, or which you were.
Is this the start or the rescue,
And which autobiographical authority. We can tame
This correspondence in eye teeth, bio.

Afternoon naps becoming harder at these endeavours: how often
You dream your responsibilities. Today's responsibility:
You cook for the family. But am I the fakest of all:
The world's new fruit rots because I am not family
When I cook, and not cooking when I am family.
But, the DNA chains, like daisy chains in our hair, drone.

Hood Wink

1

temptation to ruin the birch immediate,
deface the defensive quaintness appeared
when junior sycophant is the first receiver,
give instead the arrival motorcade
for full occupation. Le Corbusier is not far
from the tongue, but not quite on it,
wanting to be fed in that loft which constricts
his aquiline frame,
obnoxious even to the mannequins,
Stoics. Warsaw capacity for a new colony;
we can live outside in its caves, surely,
but like Virgil Thomson we are up against
a formidable genius as commander.

2

ten thirty in the tenements and there is new cubism
to the screeching face quietened by
a thronging public for the rail to Warsaw
which is by chance going there, having been Byalystock
and birch forest first. It is not liked for metaphor, so
send me to the immediate.

3

the birches are swaying, like paganism,
and all of my chill-resistant clothing is torn from me
and the miniature crows stifle the rescue
elegy of an Australian survivor and author of three
books of sentimental pseudo-autobiography.
Where might the right hagiogram be writ
to cut hagioscope from Warsaw to Melbourne,
giving me the pariah purview
to scratch hagioscope with dignity. Haworth and
Flaws in the Glass in a window which bent
but would not open. Never open maybe!
The theatre is atrocious, because unlimited,
and more brash than a keyboard, unless you touch
it with some virtual sense of innocence,
less commoditised than actual, and only
virtually might you throw off your lids.

Mercury

Encouragement towards powder and thank you owed to Mum,
she wants the shade under the coolabah we fend.
Above, and you know her better than me, the moviemaker
cultivates *South Pacific* as a sill plant – it never flowers again,
but is perennially aquamarine – which clutches at its brain for fear.

[[[!]]]

The powder grows lovingly when you pet it. It emerges as a force
in the shadow geopolitics. There is such a thing. Think about
Clive Palmer's golf course, for example, the rock collection,
dolomite, moon dust, Archimedean metals,
the spirit of mercury. But did all the kids really suck on it
to improve their personalities? Think about Cretaceous Park
and how these hands might have been archaeological instead.
Libido all the time simian, the hands felt like the feet,
and neither were ever very fast. The negative space
used to eulogise Jackson Mac Low. Everpresent cinema
as *tabula rasa*; this is pretty true. The powder
that moves with the tracing of my microscopic finger shudders,
is remorseful, it might have done a bit more about all of this.
The spaceman's teeth at the psychedelia hour, the mournful
ache of a slammed door deep in the house
when the books despise me, though patronage has come up
as a subject for conversation which the American especially
likes, which I do too, were it not for the metallic silt that

seems to build up in the dispatch when we rancour.
Books stop despising me when the powder cools, New Guinea
jungle falling into the sea, falling into pedestrian music,
falling over congratulatory boundaries. It was all so entirely
sudden, wasn't it. This encouraging hour certifies the raise
I'll gain when he remembers my face. Exquisite stupor
in the colonial-style house, guarded by palm trees.

Ecstasy

Thank you for your missing.

As I devowelled its celebration of things mutual, I swept for this new sordidality, my flies running years.

In the so kin, I erased contents now memorial, not act jewel. Permit this reply's length as it art Thames two recon suture arced cerebra Tate yon.

I add that your missing sit on a steam plume at rest in a maquette of your country lifestyle, a sweat school in a private library vaulted beside the concrete cube tomb of Cesare Battisti admired by the highest mountain in Trento, surrounded by birdsong.

I do not sleep:

Methods from Europe have
No Australian curses fearless,
Which proves at least
The inferno and duplicitous
Cuisine, you know.
I do not exaggerate.
The Catholic cringe, like youth
Again, shocks the canine
Which keeps following me.

This is good so long as the canine
Never suffers a hex by the turncoat.
Turncoat threatens me
With execution.
I can't tell you which is better,
Except that the perception
that Evil is certain is learned,
Whereas alpine living is more suspicious.
Your thousand children which
Believe the passionate love of
Language is poetry is to be expected
– where could they possibly have
Come from otherwise?
From otherwise
Is fine, I should add, and sends her
Regards.

OK, I am astronomy sometimes,
Which is a confusing
Idaho accent, but lucrative,
Because standard,
And if I quote Dorn in this accent
The audiovisual will laugh
And the constant local will groan,
But that is because
The Making of Americans remains
Mostly unread. Girt rouge stone
Is welcome retort to the canon,

Don't you think?
It's tempting never to pick up
The telephone booth again
As I slump here in a velvet lounge
With spritz and at midday,
Garda over there, the sun exciting
The water clock into the throb,
Distension, roughly
How I woke up this third time today.
That is the turbulence,
And why I adore where we are,
Which is here and not here
– your pleasure dome,
My curses recursive.

I realise this beg is full of inventions.
Last night's return dreamt a Ferris
Wheel, which is in many parts.
The triumphal mausoleum as cube
Joins the beg's caca phone.
I wonder what your thousand children
Are doing today. Surfing?
Because that is
The first thing Europeans think
Australians do, even those with
Reluctant and disputatious
Relations to a fantasy of the Union,
Like the welting truncheon televised,

For example. They're right.
Surfing is the first thing I think to do,
Though I am in fact a curse,
Incorporeal and unbalanced,
So their work on me is done.
Mausoleum as sanatorium,
Mouse scurry for sanity. Europe smiles.
Memory, keep your stasis solidly
And without smiling.
I have a right to my ecstasy.

The Person Is Real

Foam of crowd never settles but builds.
It's crazed and it's fifteen years ago. A constant moil.

These prehistoric friends, like the fig and the apricot.
The certainty that you are a person. Karratha's silence.

There was silence again near the alps, and then near the grotto.
Solar chiding wasn't there. The furious fountain of that incursion,
foam of person never settling, the unpeeling stickers of vibration.
Since it began the first rhythm can't be found any longer.
Marcel is best.
I want the conversation that is downstairs.
Wholeheartedly, beyond necessity. There are no rests
when boiling gold from sunshine.

On the frontier it is piss. That is the biblical irony
of the lonely, when you're crowded it's like a thousand breezes
lose pressure at the instant of decision. Inhalation,
today it tastes like hair and carbohydrate.

It takes twenty or twenty-five touches for the perfect family
to agree to trade with cinema, for the aspirin promised.
This model village that looks like Vienna, this computer chip,
does it make you want to empty yourself like I want to.
Mesmer's impossible RSPCA. Your cat's picture of the ideal
community made of levels, the adulturer's made of belief,

because enough will be surprised that the mall
has that much conversation,
but what about winning the lottery
in your palm
and all of the wrinkles mutinying, vibrating into a perfectly inert
electricity conductor, a virtual reflection in water,
when the dune has had enough of your suburb.

The dright that grips the hidden couch, and on the itinerary
it's really brief. No critique this hour.
I expect that groom town will keep growing the library,
then, the lifelong student will take custodianship,
the child will keep touching the engraving to check
that the person is real. Good bargain of education,
you bought us up – yes, bought! – so well.

Available for Public Events

Mandurah,
the flighty speedboats shaking terns from the pylon roost,
juveniles from the Mandurah Show and the premixes.

Drownings believed, then substantiated.
How many. Who's outdoing who, then.
Greyness, the temple's frozen passion and self-mockery,

bicentenary still about the garage sales in paraphernalia,
not monstrous, because they are heraldic,
give up their ironies easily, stand as exception

among the usual suspects.
Suspects-usury, monstrous insofar as citrus and archaeological,
not for its manners at grandad's eightieth,

for its psychedelia and heraldry. So too Mum's duplex
and the baby palm invisibly putrescent in essence.
Essence has turned to fuel.

Am I so sure you know what a duplex is, or that it has a public.

Poor Australia, he has no recognised partner or legal aid.
But he must be reassured we've rolodexed him,
the first wail, the first tantrum, which I can't affect anymore,

but can dramatise in absence as a false drowning
as the speedboat turns towards sunset
fulminating into some spectacular
Aegean public
greens and golds.

Being Paid to Live, the Dunes

You are ready for the end of this world because
you are paid for it, and the apartment is good.
If the earthquake separates the head from
the plexus, casserole.
No, the environment is more like cheese melt,
the screen a conservatory.
There are so many children born in
the depopulation zone, a great relief.
I just swallowed one accident, and another
burst in my eye. The trap is not sand
but the thugs hired to fragment
the local groundswell union,
its cities and cooperative housing,
castles and seasonal streams, are.
What emulsifies first marinates
in shadow odours of Dad.

will

The world keeps breaking in here.[4]

Your uselessness will set you free.

4 Barrett Reid, 'Art', *Making Country*, Angus and Robertson, 1995, p. 32.

Landowners have such beautiful relationships to houses,
don't they. Giddy grevilleas agree. Take charge of
bougainvillea, and the obligations of bougainvillea
to its spree enlarge, the sprawl its unabated takeover.
In the end it wins, says the distraught passionfruit.

Landowners have such beautiful relationships to
passionfruit, its consultations, and the Gold Coast boys
shiver in their collars, lighting fires, no tongues,
harry so many obsolescences collared. Farming
won't help an anxious middle and this rheumatic suburban

air, azalea.
Landowners *ad hominem*. Tenants *ad hominem*.
The fortunes of sound promising in your cheeks. *Sine qua
non* of collusion:
silence.
It would be much better if they all share-held their
very ownership, owned
their own, you know, strides the anonymous boast as beast.
Meanwhile, bougainvillea finds other ways to stockpile
your envy, some brute ruin in every dollop of road north.

Comforts in shade and warmth, the separation. Party lights,
variety in blinker, glaze over in blush heat

as tarpaulin rips by time. Lawn banishes alarm to time's drift.
  Alarm sinks.
Landowners have such relationships to landowners.

Gasp long. Furloughs from envy, quickened blood rush
  thrown far hence in a swerving citizenship.

form

A Country Practice or *Ein Landarzt*.
The betrayal is that he lay beside to comfort
and nourish the traversing child of future form.
Blood is, what, *language in the veins*
maybe. This genie gave no clue which door meant
refrigerator, which HQ, which château. It is a cold anxiety
that two families ruin in Melbourne's north.
The children will pay for this with surfeit information,
they will. In the meantime, we exhausted ourselves
with weird versions of love –
you trump at
night what you trick by day[5]
  –
Blurted all names against the wall. Aimed
at the poets, but got parties. In the archive, a boast trophy shatters.
Breakfast with love's kerosene hurts.

---

5 Javant Biarujia, '*Protasi-Apodosi pasoliniano*', *Pointcounterpoint* (Cambridge, Salt: 2007): 72.

There was a flood once in a solar change,
but I don't hope for anything.
Hope, independent of all, looks like children envying Dad's
loft today – the trick, the trump, the suspicion that we were
worthy of secrets. Then, there is transition.

By the end, hope shows all that's left.

Solo

So long as you're cool, solo lamp bends at an axis
Ataraxy. You know: the throat, minister.
I go in fear, but the youth do not and raise his body
Like an axis, which bends at his hips
And he goes soft and hangs like a towel from youth's
Shoulder, to them a palanquin, as they penetrate the Tuggerah
Wild. O but the coast, you pelicans. Wow, the pelicans.
Now that we're separated I think I am both Moreau
And the islands; more specifically, the talking rocks
Beneath the peninsula. Not arson, nor fireworks,
But the lees, rescue. I suck at drizzle. Leichhardt electorate
Aspires to a state of West.

So long as he's cool, solo lamp bends at an axis
Ataraxy. He knows: the throat, minister.
You go in fear, but the youth do not and raise my body
Like an axis, which bends at my hips
And I go soft and hang like a towel from youth's
Shoulder, to us a palanquin, as they penetrate the Tuggerah
Wild. O but the coast, pelicans. Wow, the pelicans.
Now that they're separated you think you are both Moreau
And the islands; more specifically, the talking rocks
Beneath the peninsula. Not arson, nor fireworks,
But the lees, rescue. You suck at drizzle. Leichhardt electorate
Aspires to a state of West.

So long as I'm cool, solo lamp bends at an axis
Ataraxy. I know: the throat, minister.
He goes in fear, but the youth do not and raise your body
Like an axis, which bends at your hips
And you go soft and hang like a towel from youth's
Shoulder, to all a palanquin, as they penetrate the Tuggerah
Wild. O but the coast, pelicans. Wow, the pelicans.
Now that it's separated he thinks he is both Moreau
And the islands; more specifically, the talking rocks
Beneath the peninsula. Not arson, nor fireworks,
But the lees, rescue. He sucks at drizzle. Leichhardt electorate
Aspires to a state of West.

So long as all are cool, solo lamp bends at an axis
Ataraxy. All know: the throat, minister.
All go in fear, but the youth do not and raise all body
Like an axis, which bends at all hips
And all goes soft and hangs like a towel from youth's
Shoulder, to all a palanquin, as all penetrate the Tuggerah
Wild. O but the coast, all pelicans. Wow, the pelicans.
Now that all are separated all think all are both Moreau
And the islands; more specifically, the talking rocks
Beneath the peninsula. Not arson, nor fireworks,
But the lees, rescue. All suck at drizzle. Leichhardt electorate
Aspires to a state of West.

So long as none are cool, solo lamp bends at an axis
Ataraxy. None know: the throat, minister.

None go in fear, but the youth do not and raise no body
Like an axis, which bends at no hips
And none go soft and hang like a towel from youth's
Shoulder, to none a palanquin, as none penetrate the Tuggerah
Wild. O but the coast, pelicans. Wow, the pelicans.
Now that none are separated none think none are both Moreau
And the islands; more specifically, the talking rocks
Beneath the peninsula. Not arson, nor fireworks,
But the lees, rescue. None suck at drizzle. Leichhardt electorate
Aspires to a state of West.

Afterword

The ceiling is the mattress of another bed in the bunk. Narration of an island adventure tale in Mum's voice. Bougainvillea scrapes against a narrow window, a pulse of wind drawing the thorns back and forth across the glass. Is it Sunday? Often, it seems to be Sunday. When you remember. Whose face but yours between the bars.

When I was a child, Mum read works to me from the nineteenth-century children's literature canon. *Robinson Crusoe*. *Coral Island*. *Treasure Island*. *What Katy Did*. They were all in a series. Those books came from a milk crate of books she'd bought at a garage sale. Going to garage sales was Mum's and my way to have fun on Sundays, if it wasn't sports season and if Dad didn't want to go to Fremantle. If we went to garage sales, Dad stayed home. My younger brother was always in the car with us, but he seemed more occupied with things than the journey through the suburbs of Kalamunda Shire. No one really cared what I was thinking about, or doing in that car. A great security in that. I was strangely cocooned. We'd go to Fremantle on Sundays if Dad wanted to leave the house. Crepes, waffle cones, and yellowed pages I dreamt of in the car on the way, which takes about an hour from the Hills. I dreamt of chipped porcelain, or comics, or spoilt plastic figurines if we were in the car going to garage sales. I rarely napped on these journeys, preferring to catch glimpses of the tiniest details that vehicular transport throws up. The shrouded grass tree, covered in bush litter. Collapsed marri limbs. A rabbit corpse. The corpse of a 28. Dumped computer monitor. Hub cap at an angle. Mum always bartered and we seemed to collect a lot of souvenir glassware; Dad would turn melancholy when we arrived in Fremantle, even though we had intended to be there. Both searched the Camry's seams for lost coins as we got out of the car. Hurriedly, my brother and I would slap on sunscreen.

In Fremantle, I dwelled the longest at the second-hand bookstores. I grew out of adventure stories and into macabre comics there. Elizabeth's was on a street at the end of an obscure arcade at the time, not on Market Street. Weather was always good, somehow, and this unnerved me. Mum had been reading works about cyclones, hurricanes, and typhoons in that bunk, and I preferred Gothic weather systems: haze, fog, St. Elmo's Fire. I wondered where all the meteorological action was, and why the eventful so rarely visited me. I grew to dislike the perpetually bold sky of Western Australia. Unambiguously spherical and indifferent. Icy pole blue. So obliging too, with the concomitant care of a Fremantle breeze, or a Hills evening. Most of our neighbours, family friends, and acquaintances were migrants like my parents were, often from much colder parts of the globe, and when they waxed on about the weather they swelled with adoration for this country in which I was born, and I couldn't identify with their pleasure in the least. I thought that in Western Australia we had the least imaginative weather in the whole world. Who would dream up this stupendously hypnotic, pleasant, two-tone climate, so basically hot and dry in summer and wet and cold in winter? The weather to me mirrored a self-satisfied, recreational population. The Australia portrayed on TV was worse. I found ways to escape: repetitive actions in the backyard like throwing a ball at the Hills Hoist or slapping my hands against the disused brick barbecue we had in the north corner, or hiding under tree canopies near the claypits where the national park began on one side of the suburb, or dropping rocks on slate boulders for the hollow clatter it would make. I found shroud in gossip. Fog in trivia. Everyone's front room seemed to have family history where ours was a ripple in the present.

While friends were learning solidarity (or aggression) on the football oval, visiting their big families in other suburbs, or doing their maths homework on their kitchen counter, I was (I thought) solving my parents' budget difficulties in lengthy problem-solving exercises imagined during the dull trance of a videogame on a small convex-screened TV that had to be pressed a special way to turn on. I was punishing myself in mentally staged courtroom dramas involving circular narratives about my ultimate and irresolvable lack of individual worth, I was prone, however unintentional, to ungrateful acts like breaking a hand-painted dish from Capri that my Mum's friend had given her that I knocked from a shelf when playing with my younger brother. I was imagining myself as a debate-adept adult destroying the condescension of family friends whose behaviour around my parents was transparently cruel, I thought, ever making light of their deficiencies, yet my parents didn't seem to mind having them around or visiting weekly, even praising them if they came up in conversation. I was girding myself for a life in which envy had been neutralised, because I learned through a satellite view of our family life that such a life was a cul-de-sac. Well, today I envy the ambitiousness of that stupid boy.

These were times defined by a somewhat blithe sense that life still moved forward, whether you pulled or pushed. I was a child, which made things worse. In the half-economically-conscious but always-actually-oblivious state of childhood, I was sure that it was my very biology that prevented me from recalibrating this boring trajectory forward or having any ability to reroute it. Toward what, I often thought, as 'extension on the house' and 'Disney World next year' became alley-oops of neighbourly banter. The same destinations. The same cafés. The same swimming pools. Confusingly, I had no counter-narrative from my parents to assess the value of such banter, or lack thereof. They seemed neither for nor against. I was much more concerned by the fact that everything that fascinated me was being ignored. The Rottweilers. Moreton Bay roots. The sound of rushing feet on gravel. The neighbours that never acted familiar. The graffiti on the primary school rainwater tank. The flaking foam from the armrest in a Cortina. The flavour of sourgrass pulled out of the bricks in the footpath. Pushy older brothers and sisters of acquaintances, their drugs and their wisdom. Bundies as they explode against the fibreglass of a friend's carport. Mulberry trees. Dead skin after sunburnt ears. The shell of the primary school on a Sunday. Stories of a decrepit house. The time when the bushfire came that blackened all the west-facing jarrahs near the Zig Zag. Maybe I had lots in common with other kids, or at least didn't have expectations of them. There was one kid in fourth grade whom I did dislike for his reek of adulthood, though. He had me believing that he was a detective for a whole six months. I wish I could remember this kid's name, but he moved on to another school after the only year that I knew him and I soon forgot who he was. He was one of those prematurely perverse kids who seem to know everything about the adult world and to rattle off his observations in appalling detail. I remember he said that he wagged school one day to pursue a lead which drew him back to his own house. As he approached, putting his face to the glass of the sliding door, he saw two strangers having sex in his own front room. I had vague ideas about what sex was. He informed me of what it really was. By way of this discovery, he said that he had managed to crack the case of his brother's illegal home brothel, or something like that. In the school sandpit, with its monkey bars and jungle gym, I learnt of all this detective work from a ten-year-old I had only known for a month or so. When he was about to leave, he revealed that his life as a detective had been a lie. He didn't want to ridicule me so much as to blame me. If you weren't so gullible, I wouldn't have kept fooling you, he concluded.

I had a blithe smile on my face as I dwelled on these retreating experiences and the feelings that followed them. I'm sure no no-one really knew what I was up to, and I never felt anyone would want to know, because I thought I was the only one devoted to collecting the trivia of the life of our neighbourhood. Where now we are assured that history is happening to us by the synchrony of an escalating news cycle, I remember how the aspiring cultural deconstructionist that I was in childhood thought history was always already past.

This disgusted me, and I was ashamed of my supposed immobility. The family as oriented by my parents felt like some supine satellite struggling for trajectory and ever the plaything of atmosphere. Punk had happened to my folks, for example, and I had to live in the age of its moratorium. Photos existed to confirm what I, by birth, departed from. In the 80s, my parents hung out at punk concerts in the San Francisco Bay Area when they got off work, or at least dressed like they did. There's a photo of my dad with Rowland S. Howard hair, eyeshadow, open shirt with waist showing and spandex trousers. Ever since having me, they'd given up the Bay Area and punk for the suburban Hills of WA. Traces of what's past are revealing, of course. Dad always seemed to be listening to Nirvana on Sundays when we didn't go to Fremantle, sat in the chair in the corner of the front room with those huge, world-cancelling black headphones of his. I don't remember ever being warned not to break anything in the commons of our house except those headphones. Other than the car, we didn't have anything expensive anyway, suggesting that the headphones were either expensive or precious. From a department store, my parents had bought corner lamps with movie set-style shields that could be closed over the face of the lamp, and two would always be huddled around Dad's chair, and parts of the day he would need to switch them on to get enough light in that dark corner of the house.

The case for Nirvana's *In Utero* on a brittle glass shelf beside Dad, hands in lap or biting his nails, absorbed, head lit from behind. Not a sound, except the magpies. That is Nirvana, for me, not Seattle, not existential doubt, not even nostalgia for punk.

Three years ago, for Christmas, Dad got me a mug with a photo printed into it that my Grandad took of my brother and me when I was eight and my brother was three. A strange gift, isn't it? Look at my eyes, and the width of my smile. This is a foreboding photo. My enthusiastic eyebrows are arched, like I've been prodded to perform myself. I'm so keen on making a memorable photo for Grandad, and any adult can see through the earnestness on display. We're on a track in Jorgensen Park, its ragged loveliness a sparsely chaotic Fred Williams-like background for our portrait. All the trees are caked in burn scabs. I'm smiling as if I would like to will the world to be different. But I also look artificially self-satisfied, as if I felt the decision to be happy were an achievement. Clearly, I love my brother. That's one thing I do like about this photo. I'm tucking my head into his shoulder. But, again, look at me. There's what makes this photo chilling. A fondly photographed image, with two boys staring at the lens, and one of them looks like he's trying to smile the world away.

Acknowledgements

Some of these poems first appeared in *3AM Magazine*, *Active Aesthetics* (Tuumba/Giramondo 2016), *Antipodes* (US), *Cordite Poetry Review*, *Flash Cove*, *Land Before Lines* (Hunter Publishing 2014), *Meanjin*, *Overland*, *Southerly*, *Spork Press* (US), *Vlak* (CZ), and *Writ*. 'Reform' was shortlisted for the 2015 Gwen Harwood Poetry Prize. I thank all the editors involved for their selection.

This manuscript has undergone all kinds of revision over the past few years. Many thanks to those readers of different incarnations of the book who gave such smart and unpredictable advice about these poems, and so much encouragement. Your fingerprints are cast all over the alarming conservatory. My sincere thanks to you.

Special thanks to Kevin Killian and Ann Vickery for your ludicrous praise. What were you thinking?

The Giramondo Publishing Company acknowledges the support of Western Sydney University in the implementation of its book publishing program.

This project has been assisted by the Commonwealth Government through the Australia Council, its arts funding and advisory body.